Carmen Cooks Healthy!

Represent and Solve Problems Involving Division

Martin Chilson

NEW YORK

Published in 2015 by The Rosen Publishing Group, Inc.
29 East 21st Street, New York, NY 10010

Book Design: Jonathan J. D'Rozario

Photo Credits: Cover View Stock/Getty Images; pp. 3, 4, 6, 8, 10, 12, 14, 16, 18, 20, 22, 23, 24 (blue background)AXL/Shutterstock.com; p. 4 Piti Tan/Shutterstock.com; pp. 5 (sliced orange), 9 (main) Maglara/Shutterstock.com; p. 5 (whole orange) Maks Narodenko/Shutterstock.com; p. 7 (main) Paul Orr/Shutterstock.com; p. 7 (grape) aa3/Shutterstock.com; p. 7 (banana) Svetlana Kuznetsova/Shutterstock.com; p. 9 (apple slice) KIM NGUYEN/Shutterstock.com; p. 11 (main) clearimages/Shutterstock.com; p. 11 (salsa) Dan Kosmayer/Shutterstock.com; p. 11 (pepper slice) exopixel/Shutterstock.com; p. 13 (main) Sony Ho/Shutterstock.com; p. 13 (potato pieces) Hong Vo/Shutterstock.com; p. 15 (main) julie deshaies/Shutterstock.com; p. 15 (chick pea) Charles B. Ming Onn/Shutterstock.com; p. 17 Tatiana Mihaliova/Shutterstock.com; p. 19 Joshua Resnick/Shutterstock.com; p. 21 Anna Hoychuk/Shutterstock.com; p. 22 Thomas La Mela/Shutterstock.com.

Library of Congress Cataloging-in-Publication Data

Chilson, Martin, author.
 Carmen cooks healthy! : represent and solve problems involving division / Martin Chilson.
    pages cm.— (Math masters. Operations and algebraic thinking)
 Includes index.

 ISBN 978-1-4777-4965-4 (pbk.)
 ISBN 978-1-4777-4966-1 (6-pack)
 ISBN 978-1-4777-6410-7 (library binding)

 1. Cooking—Juvenile literature. 2. Nutrition—Juvenile literature. 3. Mathematics—Juvenile literature. I. Title.
 TX652.5.C46 2015
  641.5—dc23

                              2013050402

Manufactured in the United States of America

CPSIA Compliance Information: Batch #WS15RC: For further information contact Rosen Publishing, New York, New York at 1-800-237-9932.

Contents

Food Groups

Carmen likes to stay healthy by exercising. She also stays healthy by eating good foods. She thinks it's sometimes hard to eat good foods. She doesn't always know which foods to eat or how to cook them.

Carmen's aunt is a nutritionist, which is someone who knows all about **nutrition**. She says there are 5 important food groups: fruits, vegetables, grains, protein foods, and dairy.

Carmen goes to the store to pick up **ingredients** with her aunt. She picks out 6 oranges. If Carmen divides 6 oranges into 2 groups, there are 3 oranges in each group.

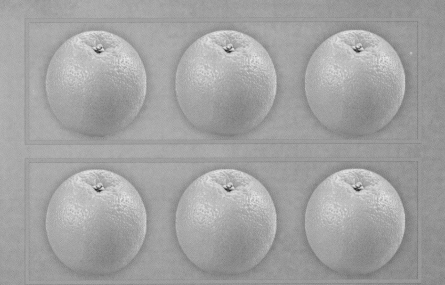

$6 \div 2 = 3$

Fun with Fruit

Carmen's aunt tells her that fruits are an important food group. They can be eaten as a snack on their own. They can also be cooked using **recipes**. Some healthy fruits are grapes, bananas, and pineapples.

Carmen wants to use the fruit they bought to make fruit salad. To make fruit salad, her aunt says to cut up all the fruits and mix them together. That's easy—but it's important to be safe using a knife!

Carmen measures a banana to be 18 centimeters and a grape to be 3 centimeters. How many grapes would she need to equal the length of the banana?

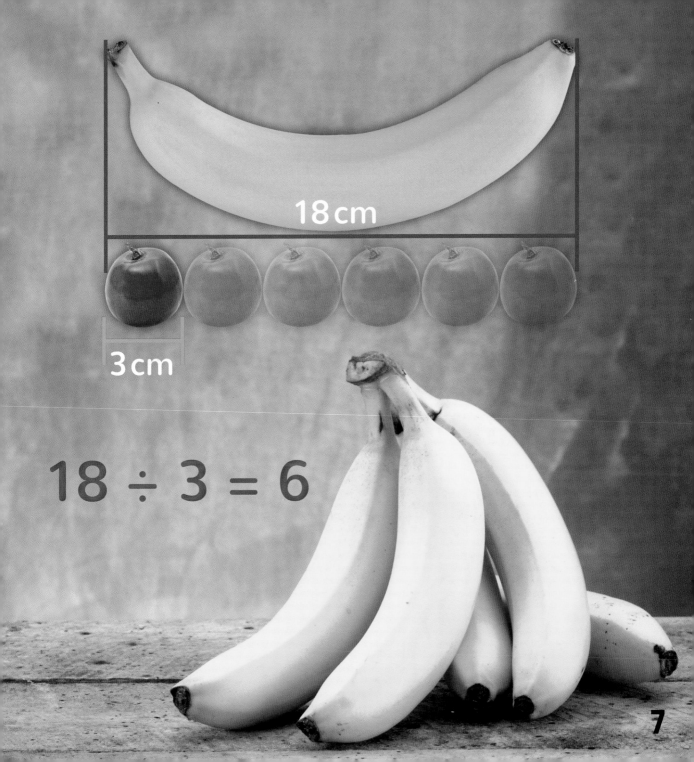

18 cm

3 cm

18 ÷ 3 = 6

Carmen's aunt says fruit can be made into yummy desserts! She wants to teach Carmen how to make applesauce. The first step is to peel the apples and cut them into small chunks.

Then, Carmen's aunt shows her how to cook the apples in a pan on the stove. She has to add a little sugar and cinnamon to keep it sweet! Applesauce can be eaten warm or cold.

Carmen has 20 chunks of apples. She divides them into 5 equal groups. There are 4 apple chunks in each group.

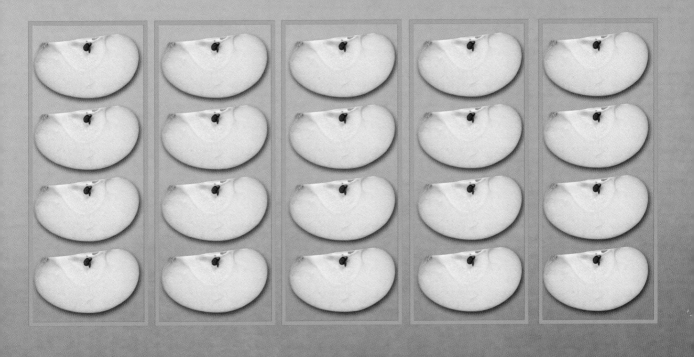

$$20 \div 5 = 4$$

9

Eating Veggies!

Like fruit, vegetables are full of important **vitamins** that keep people healthy! Some vegetables, such as carrots and celery, make great snacks on their own. All you have to do is cut them up!

Carmen's aunt teaches her how to make salsa. She needs tomatoes, onions, green peppers, and corn. Most of the ingredients in salsa are vegetables! Now, she needs to chop them and mix them together.

Salsa is a great snack! Carmen cuts her green pepper into tiny pieces. She has 28 pieces in all. If she splits these into 4 equal groups, how many will be in each group?

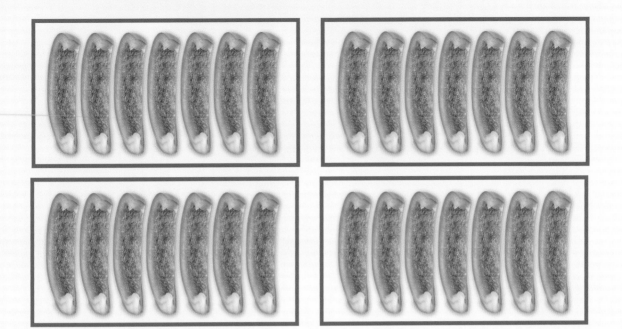

$$28 \div 4 = \text{?}$$

salsa

Carmen learns that sweet potatoes have lots of vitamins. Her aunt calls them a "superfood" because of how healthy they are.

Carmen wants to roast her sweet potatoes. First, she has to wash them. Then, she cuts them into round slices that look like coins. She adds butter, olive oil, and cinnamon. Then, she puts them in the oven. She has her aunt help because oven safety is important!

Carmen counts the sweet potato slices. There are 35 of them. She puts them into 5 equal stacks. How many slices are in each stack?

$$35 \div 5 = ?$$

13

Protein Foods

Foods with protein help build strong bones and muscles. Carmen's aunt gives her some examples of protein foods. Meat, seafood, beans, eggs, and nuts are all high in protein. Meat can come from chickens, cows, pigs, fish, and other animals.

One great example of a lean protein, or protein without a lot of fat, is the garbanzo bean. With the garbanzo bean, you can make hummus—a yummy, healthy snack!

Carmen counts out 40 garbanzo beans. She splits them into 5 groups. How many are in each group?

14

$$40 \div 5 = ?$$

15

Pass the Milk!

Dairy is any food made from milk, which has **calcium**. People need calcium to help grow strong bones. What kinds of foods are dairy foods? Carmen's aunt says milk, cheese, and yogurt are great examples of dairy.

Carmen wants to make a smoothie in a blender. Smoothies are packed with dairy and fruits, so they're healthy snacks. She uses yogurt, milk, fruit juice, and a banana. She can add other fruits, too.

$$54 \div 9 = ?$$

Carmen adds strawberries to her smoothie. She has 54 strawberries and puts them into 9 equal groups. How many strawberries are in each group?

Good Grains

Carmen learns about the last food group—grains. She knows that bread and pasta are made from grains, but what else is? Her aunt says this group includes foods made from rice, oats, wheat, and other grains. Some examples of grain foods are cereal, oatmeal, and tortillas.

Carmen's aunt teaches her to make tacos. Tacos are made of tortillas, cheese, and meat—that covers 3 food groups!

$$60 \div 10 = ?$$

Carmen's aunt has a lot of tortillas in her cupboard! There are 60 tortillas in all. If she divides them into 10 equal groups, how many are in each group?

19

It's important to eat foods that are whole grain because they're the healthiest. Foods such as white bread and white rice aren't as healthy as whole-grain bread and brown rice. It's important to choose whole-grain foods whenever you can.

Carmen's aunt is going to teach her to make spaghetti with whole-grain noodles. She heats water on the stove, and then she adds the noodles. After they're cooked, she adds tomato sauce.

$$72 \div 8 = ?$$

If Carmen has 72 noodles, how many groups of 8 can she make? Let's divide to find out!

21

Following Recipes

Carmen had so much fun cooking with her aunt! She learned how to use the blender, oven, and stove. She also learned how to peel and chop fruits and vegetables. Some recipes just call for mixing ingredients together, while others have to be cooked or baked.

While she was cooking, Carmen learned about division. It's easy to divide ingredients into equal groups. Math is an important part of following recipes!

Glossary

calcium (KAL-see-uhm) Something the body uses to build strong bones and teeth.

ingredient (ihn-GREE-dee-uhnt) Food used when cooking.

nutrition (noo-TRIH-shun) Having to do with food that's necessary for health and growth.

recipe (REH-suh-pee) A set of instructions for making food.

vitamin (VY-tuh-muhn) Something needed for the health of a body.

Index

Camels Always Do

To Doug Deming—who always makes the sisters welcome.
L.M.

To Michael
K.C

Text copyright © 2004 Lynn Manuel
Illustrations copyright © 2004 Kasia Charko

National Library of Canada Cataloguing in Publication Data

Manuel, Lynn

Camels always do / written by Lynn Manuel; illustrated by Kasia Charko.

ISBN 1-55143-284-6 (bound).–ISBN 1-55143-470-9 (pbk.)

1. Cariboo (B.C.: Regional district)–Gold discoveries–Juvenile fiction.

2. Camels–Juvenile fiction. 3. Problem solving–Juvenile fiction. 4. Picture books

for children. I. Charko, Kasia, 1949- II. Title.

First Published in the United States 2004

Library of Congress Control Number 2003116362:

Summary: What happens when an overzealous businessman imports camels to British Columbia during the gold rush?

Teachers' guide available from Orca Book Publishers.

Orca Book Publishers gratefully acknowledges the support of its publishing program provided by the following agencies: the Department of Canadian Heritage, the Canada Council for the Arts, and the British Columbia Arts Council.

Design by Christine Toller/Lynn O'Rourke
Printed and bound in Hong Kong

Orca Book Publishers
1016 Balmoral Road
Victoria, BC, Canada
V8T 1A8

Orca Book Publishers
PO Box 468
Custer, WA USA
98240-0468

PS8576.A57C34 2004   jC813'.54   C2003-907373-4

07 06 05 • 4 3 2 1

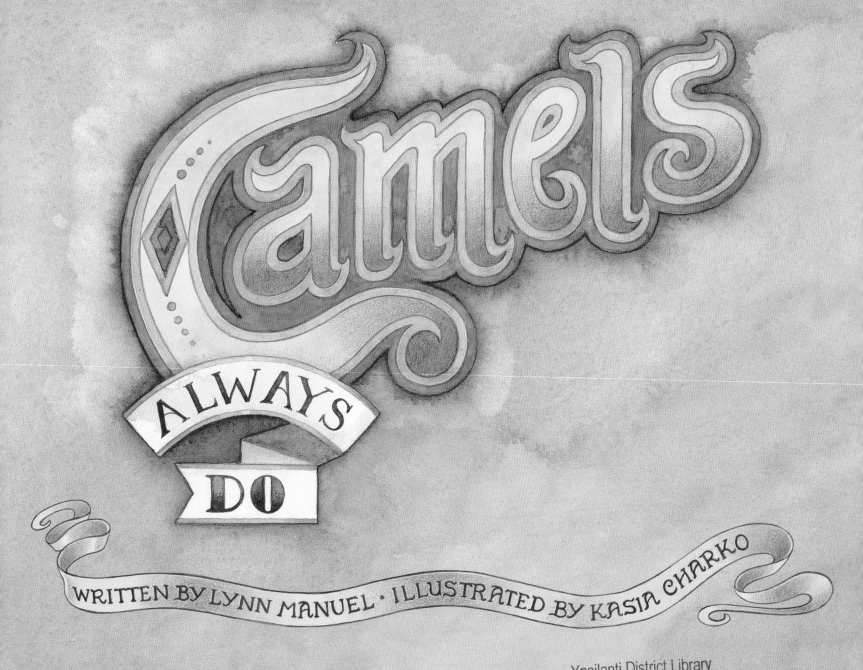

Camels

ALWAYS DO

WRITTEN BY LYNN MANUEL · ILLUSTRATED BY KASIA CHARKO

Orca Book Publishers

A long time ago there was a gold rush in the Cariboo. A boy went there with his father to look for gold. The boy's name was Cameron.

Panning for gold was a tiring job for a young boy. It took nearly all his time. When Cameron was not looking for gold, he liked to read a book he kept in his pocket, a book about camels. Cameron loved camels better than almost anything. He dreamed about visiting them in faraway places.

One evening Cameron asked, "Can we go across the ocean to see the camels?"

"Yes," said his father. "When we find gold we will see all the wonders of the world. That is something I would like to do."

Cameron worked hard helping his father. While he worked, he talked about camels. He talked about camels with one hump. He talked about camels with two humps. He talked about camels in the morning. And he talked about camels at night.

"Do camels always fill your thoughts?" his father asked him.

Cameron nodded. "Camels always do," he said.

One day when they went into town, Cameron saw something that made him blink.

Cameron saw camels. Cameron saw camels right there in the Cariboo!

The whole town was staring in wonder at the strange animals. The camels had long faces and two humps on their backs. Some were big. Some were small. There was even a baby. Cameron counted. There were twenty-one camels.

"These animals are really something!" said a man in a business suit. "Especially the big one. That Barnum has a real stubborn streak."

"Camels always do," said Cameron.

The businessman puffed his chest out proudly. "It was my idea to bring the camels here," he said. His name was Frank Laumeister. He was from Bavaria. "My partners and I paid good money for these animals. They will carry supplies to the men working in the gold fields up north."

Cameron's father was impressed. "Camels can carry big loads on their backs. They can go a long time without food and water, too."

"Yes," said Frank Laumeister. "And see those long legs? They will be able to walk through snowdrifts in the winter. The Dromedary Express is just what the Cariboo needs!"

Cameron tugged on the man's sleeve. "Mr. Laumeister, your camels have two humps. Dromedaries only have one hump."

But the man wasn't listening. "I'm looking for packers," he said. "Do you know anyone who might be interested?"

"Perhaps my son and I will take the job," said Cameron's father.

Frank Laumeister looked at Cameron. "It is a long trip to the gold fields for such a young boy."

"My son is strong," said Cameron's father. "We will manage just fine."

Frank Laumeister looked pleased. He shook hands with Cameron's father. Then he shook hands with Cameron.

The camel train made its way across the dry countryside, through the rocky canyons of the Fraser River, over Pavilion Mountain, and down to the trail followed by the fur traders.

One day Cameron noticed that Barnum was limping. Cameron and his father stopped to look at the animals' torn hooves.

"The camels do not want to walk on rocks," said Cameron's father. "They want to walk on sand."

"Camels always do," said Cameron.

"If we cannot find a solution to this problem," said his father, "the camels will not be able to deliver the supplies to the miners."

"Maybe we can make shoes for the camels," said Cameron.

"All right," agreed his father. "We can try."

So Cameron and his father set to work. They worked late into the night.

The next day the camels set out along the trail in their new shoes of rawhide and canvas.

Cameron's father was very pleased. "Today we will celebrate with beefsteak pie and onions," he said.

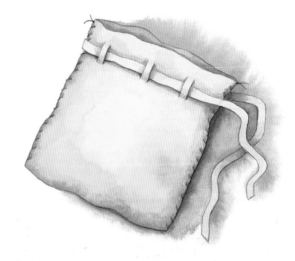

When they came to a roadhouse, a lady opened the door. She put a perfumed handkerchief over her nose. "Your camels need a bath," she said. "You cannot stop here!"

A man walked by with two mules. The mules ran away from the camels. The man chased after the mules.

"Your camels smell!" the man shouted.

"Camels always do," said Cameron.

Cameron's father said, "That is another thing that is wrong with the camels. Even animals run from their smell."

"Maybe we could give the camels a bath," said Cameron.

"All right," agreed his father. "We can try."

So Cameron and his father set to work bathing the camels in scented water. It took a very long time. The camels would not stand still.

The next day the camels set out along the trail smelling of wild roses.

After travelling through marsh and mud, the camel train finally reached Lightning Creek in the north. One night, Cameron and his father were awakened by angry shouts.

A dog was barking and chasing the camels round and round a nearby camp. Men were yelling and shaking their fists. One man was having a tug-of-war with Barnum.

"Let go of my shirt, you no-good thief!" the man shouted.

Barnum let go. The man tumbled backwards into the creek, and the big camel fired two gallons of stinky camel spit into his face.

"Aaaagh!" the man cried. "Your animals spit!"

"Camels always do," said Cameron.

Cameron's father sighed. "If the camels do not mind their manners, there's no telling what will happen."

The camels did not mind their manners. By the time they returned from the gold fields there were more angry shouts and clenched fists. The scent of wild roses had worn off. The shoes of rawhide and canvas had worn out.

Cameron and his father found Frank Laumeister surrounded by angry mule packers. The men were shouting and waving petitions.

"We do not want camels on the Cariboo trails!" hollered one man.

"I ought to sue you, Frank Laumeister!" cried another. "My mules ran away because of your camels."

"They eat everything!" bellowed a third. "Those animals eat shirts and tents and bars of soap."

"Camels always do," said Cameron.

"I guess it was not a good idea," said Frank Laumeister. "It was not a good idea to bring camels to the Cariboo."

The businessman put up a sign: CAMELS FOR SALE.

A man with a bag of gold came by.

"Do you need a camel?" asked Frank Laumeister.

"Maybe," said the man. "I will take a ride. I will see." The man sat on Barnum's back. "Get moving!" he shouted.

Barnum did not move. He did not like the man. The man climbed down. Now Barnum moved!

"Ow!" the man cried. "Your camel bit me! Those animals have bad tempers."

"Camels always do," said Cameron.

Frank Laumeister wanted nothing more to do with the camels. "Would you like to have them?" he asked Cameron.

"Oh, yes!" said Cameron. "But … I do not have any gold."

"That does not matter," said Frank Laumeister. "I will give the camels to you."

Cameron looked at the camels' sad faces and sore feet. He took off their ropes and he let them go.

"Why did you do that?" asked his father. "I thought you liked camels better than almost anything."

"Yes," said Cameron. "But I do not want them to carry big loads over the rocks."

"You are right," said his father. "It is a good thing to set them free."

But Barnum did not go far. He did not want to leave Cameron. The big camel was nearby when Cameron and his father finally found gold.

"Now we can see all the wonders of the world," said Cameron's father.

Cameron looked over at Barnum. "Is there any greater wonder than camels in the Cariboo?" he asked.

Cameron's father laughed. "Perhaps you are right," he said. "Maybe we will settle down instead, right here in the Cariboo. We will make a home for ourselves. And for Barnum, too."

"That is something I would like to do," said Cameron. And he smiled right down to his toes.

"Do camels always make you smile?" his father asked.

"Oh, yes!" said Cameron. "Camels always do."

Photo Credit: British Columbia Archives and Records Service Image #347

Although Cameron is a fictional boy, the Dromedary Express is a real part of Canadian history. In 1862, during the Cariboo gold rush, a group of businessmen led by Frank Laumeister agreed that camels would be the ideal way to transport supplies to the miners working in the gold fields of North America.

In May of that year, the Dromedary Express arrived in the Cariboo. The name itself reveals the lack of knowledge these men had about camels. Dromedaries have one hump; these camels had two. (They were in fact Bactrians.)

Perhaps if these businessmen had known more about camels, they would have realized that their venture was doomed from the very beginning.

The harshness of the Cariboo winters took its toll on the animals. And while it was true they could travel greater distances in a day with heavier loads than mules —and go much longer without food and water—camels are meant to walk on sand. Even shoes made from rawhide and canvas could not protect them from injury along the rocky Cariboo roads.

There were other problems as well, such as the unpleasant odor. Even bathing the camels in scented water was only a temporary remedy. Because of the camels' tendency to bite and kick and spit, the Dromedary Express was soon hated throughout the Cariboo. Frank Laumeister was forced to admit that his business venture was a disaster, and the camels were set free to roam the countryside.

—Lynn Manuel